DK Eye Wonder

Ocean

LONDON, NEW YORK, MUNICH,
MELBOURNE, and DELHI

Written and edited by Samantha Gray
Designed by Mary Sandberg,
Janet Allis, and Cheryl Telfer

Publishing manager Mary Ling
Managing art editor Rachael Foster
US editors Gary Werner and Margaret Parrish
Jacket design Chris Drew
Picture researcher Nicole Kaczynski
Production Kate Oliver
DTP Designer Almudena Díaz
Consultant Sue Thornton
Thanks to Sarah Walker for editorial assistance

First American edition, 2001

05 10 9 8

Published in the United States by
DK Publishing, Inc.
375 Hudson Street
New York, NY 10014

Library of Congress Cataloging-in-Publication Data

Gray, Samantha.
Ocean / by Samantha Gray.-- 1st American ed.
p. cm -- (Eye wonder) Includes index.
ISBN 0-7894-7852-8 -- ISBN 0-7894-8180-4 (lib.bdg. :alk.paper)
I. Marine animals--Juvenile literature. [I. Marine animals.]
I. Title. II. Series.
QL121.G725 2001
591.77--dc21 2001017284

ISBN 0-7894-7852-8

Color reproduction by Colourscan, Singapore
Printed and bound in Italy by L.E.G.O.

see our complete
catalog at
www.dk.com

Contents

Ocean zones

Oceans may be divided into three zones according to how far down sunlight reaches. To see which zones creatures live in, look for the red arrow in the picture below.

Schools of fish like these silver snappers swim in the sunlit zone.

Octopuses and squid live in all the ocean zones, including the twilight zone.

Sunlit zone

A red arrow pointing to the top area of this picture indicates sea creatures living in the sunlit zone. Sunlight reaches down to about 150m (450ft) deep. Most sea creatures live in sunlit water. Sunlight reaches through shallow seas and the upper waters of the open ocean.

Twilight zone

A red arrow pointing to the middle area of this picture indicates sea creatures living in the twilight zone. Light becomes dim below 150m (450ft). The twilight zone reaches from here down to about 1,000m (3,300ft) deep.

There is little food in the midnight zone, but the fangtooth's huge mouth allows it to hoover up anything that comes its way.

Deep-sea hatchet fish have lights along their bellies and tails that glow in the darkness.

Midnight zone

A red arrow pointing to the lowest area of this picture indicates sea creatures living in the midnight zone. No sunlight reaches below 3,300ft (1,000m), so the midnight zone is pitch black and extremely cold. The deepest parts of the ocean may be more than 13,200ft (4,000m) deep. This far down is known as the abyss. There are also trenches where the ocean is deeper than 19,800ft (6,000m).

Fishy facts

- The deepest ocean is the Pacific, followed by the Atlantic, then the Indian. The Arctic is the shallowest of all the oceans.

- Many sea creatures depend on ocean plantlife for their food supply. Plants need sunlight to grow.

- Coral and kelp only grow in sunlit seas.

The blue planet

Oceans cover more than two thirds of the Earth's surface. In this vast underwater world, many sea creatures live together, often hidden beneath the waves.

Gulls swoop down from the sky to scoop up a fishy snack.

Fishing for food

Oceans are a source of food for seabirds, who fly or swim in search of fish.

Sea turtles

There are many types of sea creatures, including reptiles such as turtles. These have to rise to the surface to breathe. They breathe air through their nostrils.

Green turtles live in warm waters in the Atlantic, Indian, and Pacific Oceans..

6

One big ocean

If you traveled in a boat, you could sail to every ocean and sea because they all join up. It could be said that there is really only one vast ocean.

Plankton

The sunlit ocean teems with tiny life forms called plankton. These are a vital food source for many sea creatures.

From space, Earth looks blue because water covers so much of its surface.

Breathing through blowholes

Whales are mammals. Unlike fish, they cannot breathe underwater. They surface to breathe air through their blowholes. Blue whales are the largest mammals of all.

Safety in schools
Small fish such as saupe
often swim in large groups
called schools or shoals.
There is safety in numbers!

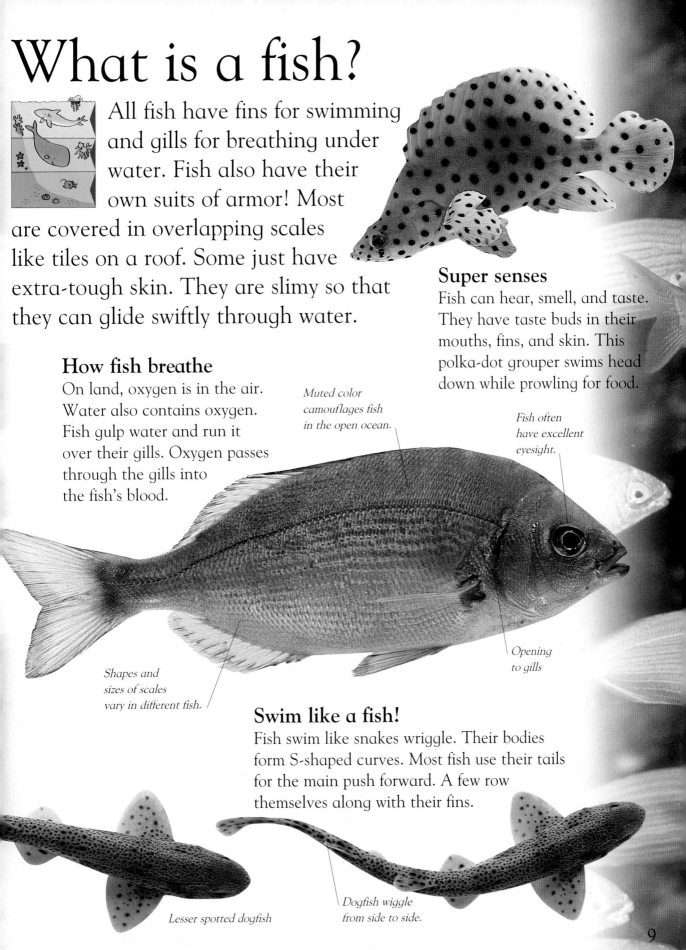

What is a fish?

All fish have fins for swimming and gills for breathing under water. Fish also have their own suits of armor! Most are covered in overlapping scales like tiles on a roof. Some just have extra-tough skin. They are slimy so that they can glide swiftly through water.

Super senses

Fish can hear, smell, and taste. They have taste buds in their mouths, fins, and skin. This polka-dot grouper swims head down while prowling for food.

How fish breathe

On land, oxygen is in the air. Water also contains oxygen. Fish gulp water and run it over their gills. Oxygen passes through the gills into the fish's blood.

Muted color camouflages fish in the open ocean.

Fish often have excellent eyesight.

Opening to gills

Shapes and sizes of scales vary in different fish.

Swim like a fish!

Fish swim like snakes wriggle. Their bodies form S-shaped curves. Most fish use their tails for the main push forward. A few row themselves along with their fins.

Lesser spotted dogfish

Dogfish wiggle from side to side.

Fantastic fish

Fish can be weird and wonderful! They vary in size from tiny sea horses to giant manta rays. Some have unusual shapes that help them to hide or scare off predators.

Manta rays flap with wide, winglike fins and glide through the water.

Prickly beauty

Lionfish have striped bodies to warn away other fish. Any predator that bites a lionfish will be pierced by poisonous spines.

Gentle giants

The vast, flat bodies of manta rays blend in with the mud and sand of the seabed. Despite their size, manta rays are gentle creatures. They eat mainly plankton.

Hidden on the seabed

Stonefish change color to blend in with the seabed. They have spines on their backs for protection. Each spine injects a deadly poison if touched.

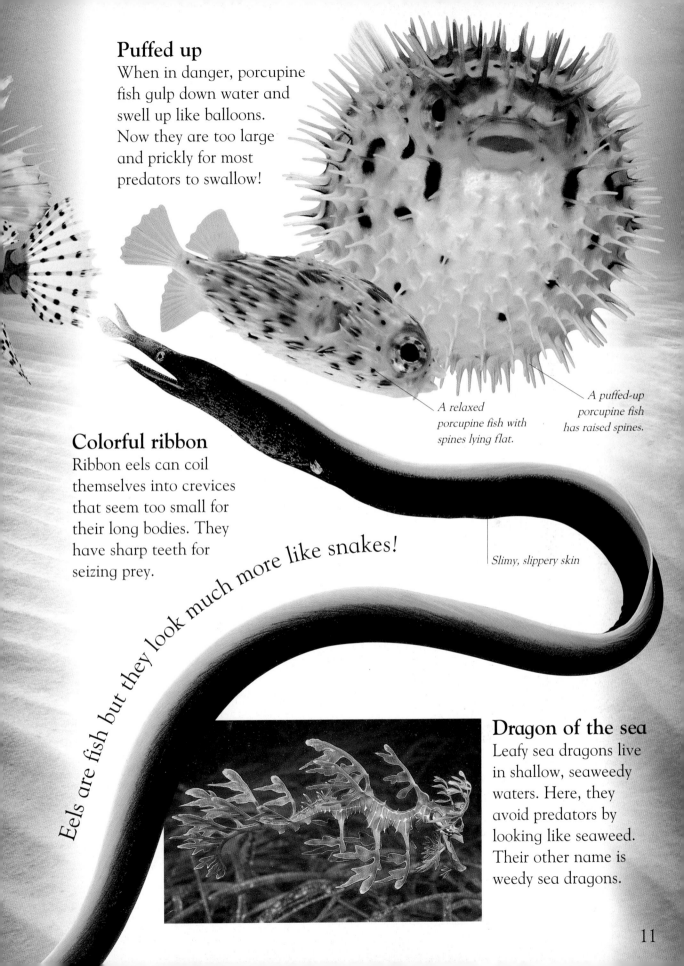

Puffed up

When in danger, porcupine fish gulp down water and swell up like balloons. Now they are too large and prickly for most predators to swallow!

A relaxed porcupine fish with spines lying flat.

A puffed-up porcupine fish has raised spines.

Colorful ribbon

Ribbon eels can coil themselves into crevices that seem too small for their long bodies. They have sharp teeth for seizing prey.

Slimy, slippery skin

Eels are fish but they look much more like snakes!

Dragon of the sea

Leafy sea dragons live in shallow, seaweedy waters. Here, they avoid predators by looking like seaweed. Their other name is weedy sea dragons.

Jellyfish

Adrift in the oceans since prehistoric times, jellyfish are more than 95% water. They have no brains, bones, hearts, or eyes. Their stinging tentacles act like fishing lines to catch prey.

Dinner delivered

Long tentacles trail from the jellyfish's body. When a small animal swims into them, the tentacles spear it with poisonous stings.

OCEAN DRIFTER

In warmer parts of the world, the Portuguese man-of-war drifts on the surface of the waves. It is held up by a balloonlike float. A relative of jellyfish, its other name is "blue jellyfish". It catches fish in its long tentacles. These shoot tiny stings into any animal that touches them. People are sometimes stung by a Portuguese man-of-war. The stings are not fatal to people, but they are very painful!

Underwater umbrella

Jellyfish have soft bodies called bells. The bell moves in and out like an umbrella opening and closing. This drives the jellyfish along.

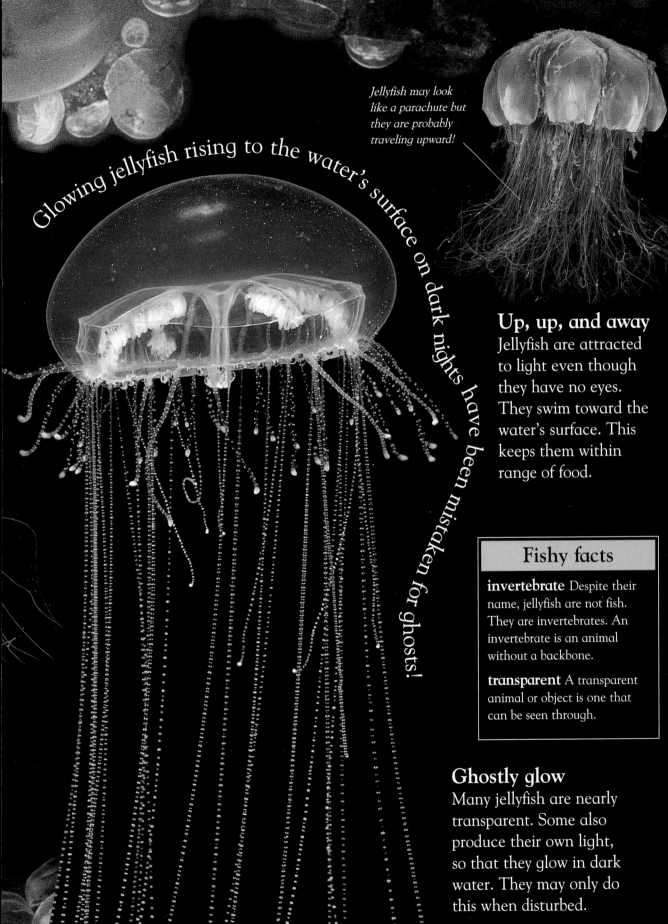

Glowing jellyfish rising to the water's surface on dark nights have been mistaken for ghosts!

Jellyfish may look like a parachute but they are probably traveling upward!

Up, up, and away

Jellyfish are attracted to light even though they have no eyes. They swim toward the water's surface. This keeps them within range of food.

Fishy facts

invertebrate Despite their name, jellyfish are not fish. They are invertebrates. An invertebrate is an animal without a backbone.

transparent A transparent animal or object is one that can be seen through.

Ghostly glow

Many jellyfish are nearly transparent. Some also produce their own light, so that they glow in dark water. They may only do this when disturbed.

Spectacular sharks

Sharks are survivors! They have lived in the world's oceans since prehistoric times. The largest of all fish, they have muscular bodies, good hearing, and a keen sense of smell for sniffing out food.

Sleek and streamlined

A strong swimmer, the sandbar shark slices through the ocean at high speed. It swims vast distances, traveling to warmer seas as seasons change.

Underwater leopards

Leopard sharks are named for their golden, spotted skin. This is good camouflage on the seabed where they search for their favorite food – clams.

Head is shaped like a hammer.

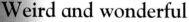

Weird and wonderful

Hammerhead sharks have eyes at each end of their unusual, wide heads. This helps them to see more! Hammerhead sharks like to stick together. There may be as many as 100 of them in a school.

World's scariest shark

Great whites are the largest carnivorous fish. Seen as ferocious man-eaters, they have been overhunted and are now rare. In fact, great whites do not hunt humans. If they do bite people, they usually spit them out!

Great whites have more than 100 razor-sharp teeth.

Ocean giants

Whales are the largest creatures in the ocean. Like all mammals, they breathe air. Whales take in air through openings called blowholes on their heads. There are two types of whales – baleen whales and toothed whales.

Splashing about

Humpback whales have longer flippers than other whales. They slap their flippers on the water to make loud splashes. This is called flippering!

Swimming lesson

A baby whale is called a calf. Humpback calves swim close to their mothers. It takes time for the calf to become a strong swimmer.

What is a baleen whale?

Humpback whales are baleen whales. Instead of teeth, they have baleen plates. They gulp water and sieve it out through the baleen, trapping tiny animals.

Killer teeth

Killer whales are toothed whales. Small, sharp teeth allow them to grab fish and other prey. Killer whales are also called orcas. They live in social groups called pods.

Leaping out of the water is called breaching.

Barnacles are small animals with shell-like plates. They often make their homes on whales.

The big blue

● The blue whale is not only the largest whale, but the largest animal of all time.

● The biggest dinosaur was only about a quarter of the weight of a blue whale.

Blue whale

Human

Killer whale

Playful dolphins

Dolphins are small, toothed whales. Intelligent and curious, they are friendly toward people. They have even rescued shipwreck survivors and helped them back to shore! Speedy swimmers, dolphins race along with long, low leaps. This is called "porpoising."

Dolphins stroke each other with their flippers to make friends.

Dolphin talk

Using a language of clicks and squeaks, pods of dolphins find their way around the ocean. They organize fish hunts by sending messages to each other. To stun fish they may make very loud noises!

Bringing up baby

Dolphins give birth to one calf at a time. The calf drinks its mother's milk and grows quickly. Other dolphins may babysit the calf while its mother hunts for fish.

Curved flippers help dolphins to steer and turn around.

Ocean acrobats

Dolphins can leap high out of the water. They may do this to avoid predators or to herd fish by making loud splashes. Males sometimes leap to impress females.

The long snout is called a beak.

Streamlined body slices through the water.

Fishy facts

● Dolphins live in groups called pods. These may join together to form a herd.

● There are dolphins in all the world's oceans, except for icy, polar waters.

● If a dolphin is sick or injured, other dolphins may support it with their bodies so that its blowhole is above the surface.

Gentle sea cows

In warm, shallow waters, large sea mammals called dugongs and manatees live a peaceful life. They have no natural enemies, eat only plants, and never fight.

Dugongs and manatees lived in the oceans during the age of the dinosaurs.

Dugongs often dig down into the sand to eat sea grass roots.

Funny face

Like manatees, this dugong has no front teeth! Its teeth grow only along the sides of its mouth. Flippers steer and scoop up food.

Noises in the night

Dugongs relax during the day and spend most of the night eating. Like manatees, they are noisy eaters. There are loud sounds of chomping teeth and flapping lips!

Manatees sometimes have algae growing on their backs.

Underwater lawnmower

Dugongs and manatees are the only vegetarian sea mammals. They swim slowly, grazing on sea grass.

Sea grass beds are good feeding grounds.

Motherly love

Dugongs and manatees give birth to only one calf every three to five years. The newborn calf rises to the surface immediately for its first breath of air. It stays with its mother for up to two years, clinging to her or resting on her back.

Calf stays close to its mother.

Fishy facts

● Dugongs have a tail that is pointed at the ends. Manatees have a paddle-shaped tail.

● On meeting, sea cows grab each other's flippers then put their mouths together to kiss.

● Manatees and dugongs can live for as long as 60 years.

Soaring seabirds

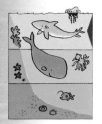

Some seabirds live along the shore. Others fly far out to sea. All return to the shore to nest. Many nest in groups called colonies. They often choose cliffs where eggs and chicks are safe from predators.

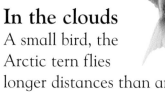

In the clouds
A small bird, the Arctic tern flies longer distances than any other bird. It spends most of its life in the air!

Wing is long and strong.

Long-distance flights
Albatrosses fly for weeks at a time. With wings outstretched, they glide through the air. They are carried by the wind and hardly need to bother to flap!

Sea parrots
Colorful beaks give puffins the nickname "parrots of the sea." Large beaks are useful for grabbing lots of sand eels!

Birds with big appetites
Pelicans fly or swim in search of a fishy meal. When they spot fish, they dive down after them. They have stretchy beaks for scooping up lots of fish in one go.

Flying underwater

Guillemots fly in long lines of up to 40 or more birds. They dive deep into the sea to snap up fish. Beating their wings, they fly through the water. Between dives, they rest and preen themselves.

Many seabirds spot fish from the sky then dive down to grab them.

Guillemots are mainly black with white chests and bellies.

Fishy facts

• Seabirds have special features for life in the water, like webbed feet for swimming.

• Water slides off their oily feathers so that they stay dry.

• Gannets and some other seabirds have extrastrong skulls. This allows them to hit the water fast in pursuit of prey.

Long-distance swimmers

Female green turtles travel to the place where they were born to lay their eggs, then swim back again across the open ocean. With no landmarks to follow, the turtles probably find their way by the positions of the Sun and the Moon.

Fishy facts

● Californian gray whales feed in the Arctic Ocean then travel to warmer waters to breed.

● Arctic terns fly further than other seabirds, from the North Pole to the South Pole and back.

● Barnacles take long-distance rides on turtles and whales.

Ocean travelers

Some sea creatures make amazing journeys, crisscrossing the oceans. They travel to find breeding grounds, food, or safety. This is called migration.

Turtles surface to breathe air through their nostrils.

Broad flippers are used for rowing themselves along.

Eels at sea
Eels travel from lakes and rivers to breed at sea. The young eels (elvers) then return to freshwater.

Lobster line up
To escape storms, spiny lobsters walk along the seabed to calmer waters. They march head to tail. This makes it hard for predators to pick out one.

Octopuses and squid

Fast hunters, octopuses and squid have long "arms" called tentacles for seizing prey. They swim at high speed by squirting jets of water from their baglike bodies. The force drives them along. This is called jet propulsion.

Sucker-studded tentacles

Octopuses feel and taste with their eight tentacles. Each tentacle has rows of suckers. The suckers help them to grip prey and fasten themselves to the seabed.

Octopuses are intelligent with large brains.

Speedy retreat

When in danger, octopuses jet off. Their bodies form a torpedolike shape to slice through water. Like squid, they can outswim most predators.

Tentacles trail out behind the body as the octopus takes off.

Nighttime prowler

In the daytime, octopuses hide alone in rocky dens. At night they come out to hunt. They try to keep a tentacle on the seabed. If threatened, they can pull themselves back fast.

Shimmering squid

Many squid can produce their own light. They use this light display to signal to each other or lure prey. Fire squid can even flash white, blue, yellow, and red light.

Ink attack!

To escape predators, octopuses and squid have a trick up their sleeves. They squirt out a cloud of ink. Hidden in murky water, they make a getaway.

Living together

Different sea creatures may live together in a variety of fascinating ways. Often the arrangement suits both creatures, but sometimes only one benefits.

A cleaner wrasse cleans the teeth of a coral trout.

Cleaning service

Fish called cleaner wrasse set up cleaning stations in coral reefs. They eat parasites stuck to larger fish. Their customers wait in line. Even natural enemies put aside their differences!

Brightly colored clown fish cannot hide easily.

Perfect partnership

Clown fish escape danger by darting into sea anemones. A coat of slime protects the fish and predators dare not follow.

Sea anemones have poisonous tentacles.

Clown fish's color and pattern warn that the sea anemone is poisonous, so both creatures benefit.

Boxing gloves

Boxer crabs carry anemones and wave the stinging tentacles at predators. Anemones eat pieces of food the crabs drop.

Food for free
Remora fish attach themselves to larger fish like sharks. They eat fragments of food that drop from their host's mouth.

Remora fish

Tangs have sharp teeth for nibbling algae.

Spring cleaning for shells
Surgeonfish such as tangs feed on algae. They sometimes nibble algae growing on turtles' shells. Turtles are glad to be cleaned up!

Down in the depths

No light reaches as far down as the ocean's midnight zone. Here, strange creatures live in freezing cold and total darkness. They are small so they can survive on little food.

Angling for fish

Angler fish have a long fishing-rod fin with a light at the end. Small fish think that this is food. Lured toward it, they swim into the angler fish's open jaws.

Stretchy stomach expands if the fish lures in a big meal.

Fearsome hunter

The viper fish swims with its jaws open. It catches fish with its extra-long, sharp teeth.

Mouth has more than 350 lights.

Low life

Parts of the ocean floor look like the surface of the Moon. Here, rattail fish dart in and out of crevices. It's easy to see how they got their name!

Ugly ogre

The gruesome looks of the fangtooth explain its other name, "ogre fish." When a fish or shrimp swims past, the fangtooth sucks them into its gigantic mouth.

Large eye helps the fish to spot prey in the dark.

Daggerlike teeth line the fangtooth's huge jaws.

Shining like stars

A bladelike, silvery body gives hatchet fish their name. They have light organs along their bellies and tails.

Life on the seabed

A few seabed animals can survive along the lower seashore. Most live on the deeper seabed where they are always underwater. These creatures often look like plants but they are really animals.

Sponges can grow so big that a person could have a bath in one!

Sponges attach themselves to the seabed.

Seabed chimneys

Sponges come in strange shapes and many colors. They feed by capturing plankton as they pump water through their bodies.

Spines cover body and arms.

Starring role

Brittle stars have brittle, easily broken arms. This does not matter because they can grow new ones! Like starfish, brittle stars do not have a brain.

This common starfish has 12 arms.

Hungry starfish

Starfish eat mussels and clams, using the suckers on their feet to pull the shells apart. Then they push their stomachs into the gap and eat up their prey.

Pair of tentacles helps sea slugs seek out food.

Tentacles can be pulled back inside the body.

Row of feet

In the slow lane

Sea cucumbers crawl along the seabed at a snail's pace. They suck in food that sticks to their slimy tentacles.

Colorful character

This sea slug is called a "Spanish shawl" because it appears to have an orange fringe. The vivid colors of sea slugs warn predators that they are poisonous and taste awful.

Fishy facts

● Coral reefs grow in tropical oceans where sea temperature is never below 68°F (20°C).

● Australia's Great Barrier Reef is so large that it can be seen from space.

● New coral reefs will often grow on the seabed wrecks of ships and aircraft.

Coral reefs

Coral is built by tiny animals called polyps. Each builds a chalky, cup-shaped shelter to protect its soft body. The reef spreads as young polyps build new shelters on old ones. Different corals form a variety of amazing shapes and colors.

Organ pipes

A new layer of coral grows from each tiny pipe of organ-pipe coral.

Rose coral

Corals have names that tell you how they look. This coral is like a rose.

Scallops often make their home in rose coral.

Sea fans

The treelike forms of these corals sometimes join up in the shape of a fan.

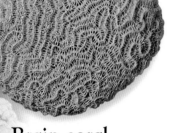

Brain coral

Brain coral is a grayish color and looks like a human brain!

Colorful coral reefs look like underwater gardens.

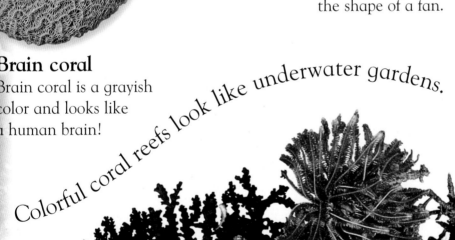

Life in a coral reef

Coral reefs teem in the daytime with beautiful and bizarre creatures. At night, many retreat into caves to rest. Now a new party begins! Different fish leave their hideouts to look for food.

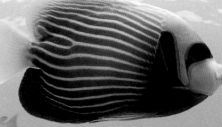

Underwater angels

With their slim bodies, emperor angelfish can dart in and out of gaps in the coral. Angelfish partners stay together for life.

SEA SERPENT STORIES

Tales of man-eating sea serpents once made people wary of eels. Today, divers still tell stories of moray eels gripping them in their toothy jaws. Divers mostly have only themselves to blame. Some poke their hands into coral-reef caves. This can give an eel resting at home an unwelcome surprise!

Lettuce leaf
Like other sea
slugs, lettuce
slugs are related
to garden snails.
These frilly slugs
may look like salad, but
their skin produces a slime
that tastes revolting.

Coral reefs
offer many
hiding places
for small fish
escaping from
larger predators.

A twist of the tail
To anchor themselves, sea
horses twist their tails
around coral. If an
enemy appears, they
change color
to match their
surrounding.

*Sea horses are
among the
tiniest fish in
a coral reef.*

Slippery as an eel
Moray eels have slimy, snakelike
bodies. They slither into caves and
crevices to hide during the day.
Their pointed faces peer out from
the coral. At night, they hunt
for food.

House-hunting hermits
Hermit crabs often make their
homes inside the empty shells
of other animals. They may
also move into small caves in
the coral reef.

Icy waters

The seas around the North and South poles are partly frozen. Animals that live here have a thick layer of fat, called blubber. This helps to keep them warm.

Coming up for air

Like all mammals, seals breathe air. They gnaw at sea ice with their sharp teeth to keep open air holes for breathing.

Pups are completely covered in white fur.

Snow-white seal pups

Harp seal pups are born with white fur that camouflages them on the ice. This is useful because they often wait alone for their mothers to return from feeding.

Polar bears have black skin under their white fur.

Noisy walruses

Walruses live in large groups around the North Pole. These noisy animals bark, growl, and whistle to each other. They have two long front teeth called tusks.

A walrus's tusks can grow up to 3ft (1m) long.

Fishy facts

● Harp seal pups drink their mothers' milk for about two weeks, then find their own food.

● Growing up to 10ft (3m) high, polar bears are nearly twice as tall as a person.

● Polar bears build snow dens to shelter their cubs. They always have twins!

Swimming under ice

Polar bears hunt prey in icy Arctic seas. Their slightly webbed toes help them to swim. They paddle with their front legs and steer with their hind ones. In the snow, creamy fur is perfect camouflage.

Penguin party

All penguins live south of the Earth's equator. They have thick fat called blubber to keep them warm in icy waters. Shiny, waterproof feathers prevent their skin from getting wet. They make deep dives to catch fish.

Daring divers

Adélie penguins are the most common South Pole penguins. They dive into the icy water to hunt for fish and squid. Swimming at high speed, they can launch themselves from the water onto the shore.

Streamlined shape slices through water.

Flipperlike wing rows penguin along underwater.

Webbed foot has claws.

Fishy facts

- Penguins can dive down to about 870ft (290m), taking them into the twilight zone.

- The emperor penguin is the largest penguin of all.

- Many penguins live in the coldest, windiest place in the world – the South Pole.

Making a splash

Penguins are speedy swimmers, but they have no defense against predators. In water, their dark backs and light-colored bellies act as camouflage. This is known as countershading.

Penguins are birds but they cannot fly. They waddle slowly on land but swim swiftly in the sea.

Dinner is served

Penguin parents feed their chicks fishy snacks until the chicks can hunt for themselves. Emperor penguin chicks have gray, fluffy feathers. Later, they grow black and white feathers like their parents.

Perfect parent

After laying eggs, female king penguins return to the sea. Through the icy winter, the males keep the eggs warm on their feet. When the chicks hatch, their mothers reappear to feed them.

Nursery on the ice

Emperor penguin chicks and adults huddle together in groups of up to 5,000 birds. It is much warmer inside the huddle than outside it. Penguins move around slowly, so that those on the outside have a turn in the middle to warm up!

Kelp is a type of giant seaweed, and the largest of all ocean plants.

Super snacks

Kelp attracts schools of small fish. This does not go unnoticed by harbor seals. They can scoop up a good meal, then relax in the canopy of kelp leaves near the water's surface.

Roaring sea lions

Sea lions get their name from roaring like lions. They also bark and honk. In the kelp, they search for clams, crabs, fish, and lobsters to eat. They are fast swimmers, with winglike front flippers.

Kingdom of kelp

Hidden under the waves, kelp forests provide food and shelter for a wealth of creatures. A towering kelp plant is like a high-rise apartment, providing homes for sea creatures at every level.

Hanging out in hammocks
Sea otters lie in hammocks of kelp. Their waterproof fur is so thick that their skin never gets wet! They use their stomachs as a table for laying out meals.

Some fish graze on the kelp, while others hunt for prey.

Forest flame
Flame-colored garibaldis have small territories in the kelp. If a neighbor gets too close, the garibaldis confront each other face to face. They wave their tails furiously.

Shady shark
Horn sharks hunt for sea urchins and shellfish at night. Their eyes are sensitive to light, so they sleep during the day in the shade of large kelp leaves.

Kelp is attached to the seabed by rootlike anchors called holdfasts.

Exploring under water

Oceans have yet to be fully explored. They still have secrets to reveal. To survive under water, divers need special clothing and equipment. Today, they can also travel in under water machines called submersibles.

Scuba diving

Scuba (Self-Contained Under-water Breathing Apparatus) allows divers to breathe from tanks of air strapped to their backs.

Scuba divers study fish and the seabed in shallow waters.

BUBBLE TROUBLE

Scuba equipment allows divers to study shallow-water fish in the wild. The problem is that fish like hammerhead sharks are sensitive to the noise made by air bubbles. They may be so scared that they swim away.

Diving machines

Submersibles are the only way to explore the deep ocean. In them, divers have discovered undersea life never seen before. They are protected from the huge pressure of water that occurs at low levels. The submersible *Nautile* can dive to nearly 20,000ft (6,000m).

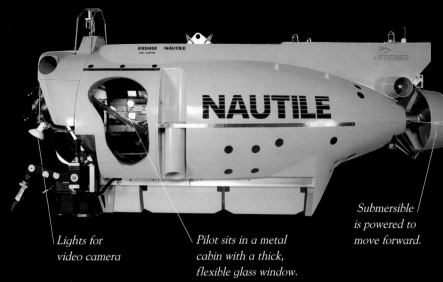

Lights for video camera

Pilot sits in a metal cabin with a thick, flexible glass window.

Submersible is powered to move forward.

Diver studying a shipwreck on the seabed.

Seabed wrecks

Shipwrecks come to rest on the seabed. Scuba divers can explore them in shallow seas. Here, algae and sometimes coral grow on the wrecks as time passes.

Disaster in the Atlantic

In 1912, the *Titanic* hit an iceberg and sank on its first-ever voyage. The advent of submersibles meant that the wreck could finally be explored. *Nautile* took nearly two hours to reach it.

Glossary

Algae plants that live in water. They have no roots, stems, or leaves. Seaweed is a sea algae.

Animal an animal is any living creature that is not a plant. For example, dolphins, fish, and starfish are animals.

Antarctic the cold area around the South Pole, which includes the southern parts of the Atlantic, Indian, and Pacific oceans.

Arctic the cold area around the North Pole, which includes the Arctic Ocean.

Baleen baleen is made of the same material as human fingernails. Some whales have baleen plates instead of teeth.

Blubber a thick layer of fat that keeps polar animals and whales warm in cold waters.

Breeding when animals give birth to young.

Camouflage for animals, this is usually skin coloring that makes them look the same as their surroundings. They are then less likely to be attacked.

Canopy the topmost layers of leaves in a forest. Kelp forests have a canopy.

Carnivore an animal that eats the flesh of another animal.

Coast the border of the land where it meets the sea.

Continental shelf the shallow part of the seabed around land that ends in a steep slope to the ocean floor.

Countershading this is the effect of having a darker back and paler belly. From above, a dark back blends in with the darkness of the deep sea. From below, a pale belly blends in with the light from the sky.

Crustacean a type of animal with jointed limbs. Crabs, lobsters, and shrimp are examples of crustaceans.

Echinoderms animals with spiny skins and tubed feet. Sea cucumbers, sea urchins, and starfish are echinoderms.

Equator an imaginary line around Earth that is equally distant from the North and the South poles.

Gills the part of a fish's body that absorbs oxygen from water so that fish can breathe under water.

Holdfast the rootlike anchors attached to kelp.

Invertebrate an animal without a backbone.

Kelp a type of giant seaweed.

Luminous this describes the effect of giving off light. Some fish have light organs that make them luminous.

Mammal a warm-blooded animal that breathes oxygen from the air. Female mammals produce milk to feed their young.

Mollusc animals that have a soft body and no backbone. Clams, octopuses, sea slugs, and squid are molluscs.

Oceanography the study of the oceans is called oceanography.

Oxygen a gas that is found in both air and water. All living things need oxygen to breathe.

Parasite an animal that lives in, or on, another animal. A parasite benefits at the expense of the other animal.

Plankton tiny plants and animals that live in the ocean. They are food for many other, larger sea creatures.

Polar region the area near the North Pole or the South Pole.

Predator an animal that hunts other animals for food.

Prey an animal that is hunted by other animals for food.

Scale a small, thin plate. Overlapping scales protect the skin of fish and reptiles.

Sea smaller areas of saltwater are called seas. Larger areas of saltwater are called oceans.

Species a group of animals or plants made up of related individuals who are able to produce young with one another.

Seashore the land along the edge of seas and oceans.

Streamlined a smooth shape that allows some sea creatures to travel faster.

Submersible a diving machine for exploring the deep ocean.

Tentacles long feelers, like bendable arms, for grasping.

Territory an area defended by an animal, or animals, against others of its kind.

Animal alphabet

Every animal pictured in this book is listed here, along with its page number and the parts of the ocean in which it lives.

Index

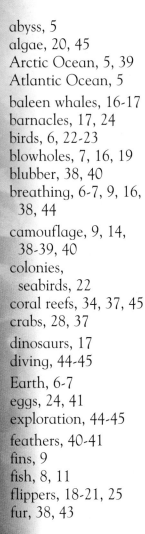
Acknowledgments

Dorling Kindersley would like to thank: Hilary Bird for compiling the index, Emily Bolam for original artwork, Penelope York for editorial assistance, and Jon Hughes for additional design work.

Picture credits:
(Key: a = above; b = below; c = center; l = left; r = right; t = top)
Dorling Kindersley would like to thank the following for their kind permission to reproduce their photographs / images:

Bruce Coleman Ltd: 6c, 11bc; Andrew Purcell 8c, 9r; Charles and Sandra Hood 12r, 43bc; Dr Eckart Pott 41bl; Dr Frieder Sauer 12bl; Fred Bruemmer 38c; Gordon Langsbury 22tr; Hans Reinhard 41br; Jeff Foott 33br, 42c; Joe Mcdonald 6tl; John Cancalosi 22bl; Johnny Johnson 22ac; Mark Carwardine 17tl; Mark Cawardine 7br; Pacific Stock 4c, 14tc, 14br, 14b, 14l, 15c, 16b, 16t, 26c, 27ac, 32t, 33cr, 42br, 44c, 46c; Steven C Kaufman 38br. **DK Picture Library:** Frank Greenaway 14cl; Jerry Young 48tr. **Robert Harding Picture Library:** John Warden 39c. **N.H.P.A.:** 13cl; Bill Wood 28tl; Norbert Wu 29tl;

Robert Wu 30tl. **Oxford Scientific Films:** David B. Fleetham 13tr, 20cl; Doug Allan 23c; Herb Segars 12tl; Howard Hall 12br, 13t, 18c, 25br; Konrad Wothe 19tr; Laurence Gould 45c; Paul Kay 32b; Peter Parks 30clb; Tamy Peluso 27br; Tobias Bernhard 20cr. **Pictor International:** 4l. **Planet Earth Pictures:** 34c, 35bc, 35r, 36c, 37r; A. Kerstitch 33tl; Ashley J. Boyd 37b; David Seiferi 18bl; Doug Perrine 29c; Gary Bell 2l, 3r, 28bl; Mark Conlin 20b; Norbert Wu 31bc, 43ac; Pieter Folkens 38tr; Tom Walker 17tr. **Science Photo Library:** Art Wolfe 40c, 41tr; Douglas Faulkner 21c; F.S. Westmorland 1c. **Southampton Oceanography Centre:** 30b. **gettyone stone:** George Lepp 22br. **Telegraph Colour Library:** 10c.

Jacket: **Bruce Coleman Ltd:** Pacific Stock 10000bl. **Oxford Scientific Films:** Howard Hall 10001c; Mark Webster 10000br.

Useful website addresses:
EnchantedLearning.com/subjects/ ocean; www.aqua.org; www.underwater.com.au; www.ocean.udel.edu/deepsea/.